SPEECH

OF

JAMES O. PUTNAM,

OF BUFFALO,

ON THE BILL, PROVIDING FOR THE

VESTING OF THE TITLE OF CHURCH PROPERTY IN LAY TRUSTEES.

DELIVERED IN THE SENATE OF NEW YORK,

JANUARY 30, 1855.

For who knows not that Truth is strong, next to the Almighty; she needs no policies, nor stratagems nor licensings, to make her victorious; those are the shifts and the defences that error uses against her power.—MILTON.

ALBANY:
VAN BENTHUYSEN, PRINTER, 407 BROADWAY.
1855.

SPEECH.

Mr. CHAIRMAN:—As I originally introduced, and subsequently reported this bill from the select committee, without stating at length their views, it seems proper that I should submit to the Senate the objects at which it aims, and the considerations which have induced my action. The bills seeks uniformity in the tenure of church temporalities. While my attention has, as a legislator, been called to the questions involved, I have been sensible of the importance of maintaining to all citizens of every shade of religious sentiment, the constitutional guarantee of the "free exercise and enjoyment of religious profession and worship." While I believe this principle is in no measure violated by the bill proposed, I remember that even this guarantee, is made by the fundamental law, subject to the condition, "that it do not lead to practices inconsistent with the peace or safety of the State." *Salus populi, suprema lex*, is the paramount idea of the Constitution. This bill interferes with no belief, it strikes at no general and long established policy of any church, or of any body of religionists. It simply provides for the vesting of the title of lands dedicated to religious uses, in Trustees of the congregation enjoying the same, in accordance with a law and policy of the State which are almost co-existent with its incorporation into the Federal Union. It may lead us to a better appreciation of this subject if we refer to that policy, and to the motives which led to its adoption.

The organization of New York, like that of her sister colonies, into a free and independent State, was the result of the triumph of the popular principle of the right of man to self government.

That organization was the overthrow of all political power not emanating from the popular will, and of all undue prerogative on the part of a priesthood. New York, as she shared its labors and sacrifices, fully sympathized with the spirit of the Revolution, and has ever adhered to the Republican policy in all matters pertaining to Church or State. If the founders of our State government were careful to secure to the people the right of governing themselves, and to throw around the citizen the safeguards of a constitutional liberty, they were no less careful to confine the clergy within their legitimate sphere as spiritual guides. This jealousy of clerical influence is one of the most marked features of our first State Constitution. Let us look for a moment at the rock from which we were hewed. It is well, at times, to trace the stream back to its fountain.

The preambles of sections 38 and 39, of our first State Constitution, which are declaratory of the free exercise of religious liberty, are as follows:

38. And whereas we are required by the benevolent principles of rational liberty, not only to expel civil tyranny, but also to guard against *that spiritual oppression and intolerance* wherewith the bigotry and ambition of weak and wicked *priests* and princes have scourged mankind, this convention doth, &c., (declaration of free exercise of religion, here follows.)

39. And whereas the ministers of the gospel are by their profession, dedicated *to the service of God and the cure of souls, and ought not to be diverted from the great duties of their function*, therefore no minister, &c., (concludes with a declaration of their ineligibility to any civil or military office.)

Thus it appears that at the very origin of our State government, when was settled the policy which should exist for ages, with such modifications as a progressive civilization, and an advancing sentiment of liberty might require, our fathers recorded their experience of past oppressions under priestly rule, and declared it to be their conviction that the safety of the State from "spiritual oppression and intolerance," depended upon the limitation of the authority of the clergy to what they might legitimately acquire in their office as spiritual teachers. Very soon after the adoption of the Constitution, and in 1784, the Legislature was called upon to form a system of government of church temporalities, and one was carefully perfected in entire harmony with the theory of our political Institutions.

Leaving the clergy 'to the service of God and the cure of souls,' they secured the independence of the laity, and the rights of conscience, by the most practical limitation of the power of the priesthood, which could be obtained by legislation. The act of 1784 "to provide for the incorporation of religious societies," and which is substantially the act under which all church property until very recently has been held, provided that the title of such property should be vested in Trustees elected by the church, congregation or society, occupying and using the same, for purposes of religious worship. Slight modifications of that act have been made to meet the practice of two or three denominations of Christians, but none of them yielding the great principle that the laity should have the substantial control of the property, through their representatives elected by the body of the church or congregation. This develops to us the policy of the State, and the constitution from which we have quoted, reveals the considerations which led to its adoption.

It is a policy alike cautious and Republican. It recognizes the justice of placing the control of consecrated property in the hands of those by whose sacrifices and bounty it was acquired. It manifests that jealousy of the power of the priesthood, not necessarily incident to their spiritual office, which their own experience, as well as the history of centuries of contest, between the clergy and the laity, could not but awaken. This act secured the rights of conscience and the freedom of worship. It realized a central idea of the revolution—a separation of church and State. It was a practical embodiment of the American sentiment. "A PRIEST FOR THE PEOPLE, AND NOT, THE PEOPLE FOR A PRIEST."

Under this act, all the religious societies of the State soon organized. Protestant and Catholic alike, availed themselves of its provisions, and the line of demarkation of power between the clergy and the laity contemplated by the constitution, and defined by this enactment, has been carefully preserved until the last few years. If it sometimes facilitated a change of dogmas in the faith of worshippers of a particular congregation, it has been supposed that what was lost to a self-claimed orthodoxy, was more than gained to the rights of conscience and the freedom of inquiry.

Under this Republican policy, the different denominations of Christians have grown powerful in numbers and influence, without any abatement on the part of the people of respect for their spiritual teachers. On the contrary, by divesting the clergy of all power over church temporalities, and thus removing a cause of jealousy and strife, unhappy collisions have been avoided, and they have lived as the spiritual guides and the friends of their people, who in turn, have reposed in them that confidence, and yielded to them that esteem, which belong to consistent piety, and to useful lives.

Within the last few years has grown up in this State, a system of rule entirely antagonistic to the system I have reviewed, and in violation of the whole spirit of our constitution and laws. This is its history. As early as 1829, it was discovered by the Prelates of the Catholic Church, that under American institutions, the system of committing the control of church temporalities to the laity, led to a degree of independence of the priesthood, not in keeping with the absolutism of the Catholic Hierarchy. Its tendency was to divide power with the clergy. To meet this difficulty, the following ordinance was passed in the Grand Council of Bishops, held at Baltimore, Oct. 1, 1829:

"*Council of Baltimore, Oct.* 1, 1829.

"Whereas lay trustees have frequently abused the right (*jure*) granted to them by the civil authority, to the great detriment of religion and scandal of the faithful, we most earnestly desire (*optamus maxime*) that in future no church be erected or consecrated unless it be assigned by a written instrument to the bishop in whose diocese it is to be erected for the divine worship and use of the faithful, whenever this can be done.

"Approved by Gregory XVI, Oct. 16, 1830."

This, it will be observed, was expressive of no more than an earnest desire. It was an appeal to the *amiability* of the Catholic congregations.

That appeal failed of its purpose, and so much were the people disinclined to comply with this policy, when not urged as a *right*, that another step was taken in 1849, at the seventh Provincial Council of Bishops of the United States held at Baltimore, when a measure of revolution was adopted, no less than the divesting of the Catholic laity of all power over Church temporalities, and its centralization in the hands of the priesthood.

The fourth article of the ordinances of that Assembly, is as follows:

"Article 4. The Fathers ordain, that all Churches, and all other Ecclesiastical property, which have been acquired by donations or the offerings of the Faithful, for religious or charitable use *belong* to the bishop of the diocese; unless it shall be made to appear, and be confirmed by writings, that it was granted to some religious order of monks, or to some congregation of priests for their use."

This is no less than an act of confiscation. It does not even recognize the right of property in those by whose bounty it was purchased, but it arrogates to the Bishops an *actual proprietorship*, and by *absolute* decree of this ecclesiastical council, so far as it could be enforced by persuasion or discipline, transfers the possession, control, and ownership, of millions of property, from the laity, to the clergy.

This was a policy on the part of the Catholic clergy, no less bold in its antagonism to the whole theory of our government, than happily adapted to the objects of control at which it seems to have been aimed.

It may be added, that this ordinance was submitted to, and received the approval of, the Pope of Rome.

Immediately upon the promulgation of this new order, the bishops in their respective dioceses throughout the United States, commenced the effort to obtain the surrender of all corporate churches on the part of their congregations, and the transfer to them individually, of the titles to church property, cemeteries, seminaries of learning, hospitals, &c., &c. In most instances in this State, it being made a test of good Catholicism, these transfers were made without protracted resistance. In other instances, among congregations imbued with the spirit of our free institutions, and who had learned to recognize as just, the division of power between the clergy and the laity, which our civil polity had established, this demand was resisted. The Catholic laity claimed that their rights did not exist by mere sufferance of the clergy. That having organized into Corporations in pursuance of our laws, they were bound as good citizens to abide by the policy of the government whose protection they enjoyed. When this resistance was protracted, it led to the most unhappy controversies. And wherever the congregations have finally refused to yield their franchises, and surrender their titles in obedience to the Baltimore ordinance, they have suffered the severest penalties which can, in this country, be inflicted upon the Catholic communicant. The church of St. Louis, in the city of Buffalo, is one of the congregations which have adhered to the policy of the State. This congregation is composed of a French and German population, most of whom have been for many years residents of the United States.

Their petition to this body details an unhappy controversy of several years. The real estate upon which their church edifice was erected, was in 1829 conveyed for the use of a Catholic congregation to be thereafter organized, by the late Louis Le Couteulx, a man most honorably associated with the history of his adopted City and State. In 1838, the congregation was organized under the laws of this State, and seven trustees elected, in whom the title vested by virtue of the act in relation to religious corporations. Before the passage of the Baltimore ordinance, Bishop Hughes "attempted to compel the trustees to convey the title of this church property to him." After the Baltimore ordinance were vigorous measures were set in operation by the Bishop of that diocese, to compel the transfer of the title. A son of the grantor of the land made a visit to the Head of the church at Rome, to obtain an equitable adjustment of the controversy. The result was, the deputation of Arch Bishop Bedini, a Nuncio of the Pope, to visit the church, and if possible, settle its difficulties. The Nuncio refused any terms, except those which had been previously made by the Bishop, in compliance with the Baltimore ordinance, and transfer of title. In September last, the Bishop made his final proposition for an adjustment, which was rejected.

For this adhesion to our laws on the part of the St. Louis congregation, their trustees have been excommunicated. Every sacrament, every sacred privilege most dear to the sincere Catholic, have been denied the members of the congregation.

In their petition they say:

"For no higher offence than simply refusing to violate the Trust Law of our State, we have been subjected to the pains of excommunication, and our names held up to infamy and reproach. For this cause, too, have the entire congregation been placed under ban. To our members the holy rites of baptism and of burial have been denied. The marriage sacrament is refused. The Priest is forbidden to minister at our altars. In sickness, and at the hour of death, the holy consolations of religion are withheld. To the Catholic churchman it is scarcely possible to exaggerate the magnitude of such deprivations.

"We yield to none in attachment to our religion, and cheerfully render to the Bishop that obedience, in spiritual matters, which the just interpretation of our faith may require; but in respect to the temporalities of our Church, we claim the right of obeying the laws of the State, whose protection we enjoy."

While the Bishops have been securing the transfer to themselves of the title of church property consecrated at the time of the action at Baltimore, they have taken in every instance in this State, so far as I can ascertain, the title of all property which since that action has been purchased for church, educational, or charitable purposes, in connection with the Catholic communion. In the county of Erie alone, nearly sixty different conveyances of lands, have been made to John Timon, the Bishop of the Buffalo diocese, during the last seven years, and the value of this property is estimated at over one million dollars. This property consists of sites of churches, cathedrals, hospitals, and educational establishments, besides a large amount of yet vacant lands. Some estimate may be formed of the vast aggregate of property now vested in the three Catholic Bishops of New York, from this statement in relation to a single county which contains but one city, and that having but seventy thousand inhabitants. The legal effect of this proprietorship in the Bishop, is to vest the absolute title in him as an individual, so that were he to die intestate, it would go to his heirs. But it is presumed that he lives with an executed will, which devises his property, to his successor in office, thus practically creating a close corporation sole, in the Bishop of the diocese.

This then is the present position of this question.

Our Constitution and policy are Republican.

The State guarantees the freedom of worship and the liberty of conscience to all its citizens. As a part of its policy, and to prevent that undue influence of the priesthood over the people which is alike incompatible with the personal freedom of the citizen, and with the safety of the State, it has engrafted the popular element upon the system of rule in church property.

The State finds a counter policy in the Catholic Church. Its democratic system is met and antagonized by the absolute element, of a spiritual power defiant of all our usages and laws.

It finds millions of property, wrested from the hands of congregations, and concentrated in individual ecclesiastics.

It finds a priesthood, not content with the legitimate influence which belongs to their character as spiritual guides, securing a power over timid consciences, little less than absolute, through their control over every consecrated place.

It finds this system of rule creating bitter dissensions, between priest and people, dangerous to the peace of society.

It finds itself called upon by Catholic congregations, whose only crime is, that they have obeyed the laws, to interpose between them and these ecclesiastical exactions.

Has the State a duty to perform in view of these facts?

What, Sir, will the State answer to the church of St. Louis, and other congregations sympathizing with it, whose sufferings for adhering to our laws are so forcibly depicted in their petition? To say nothing of the great principles involved in this question, on which side should be found the sympathy of the government. With those who seek to establish a policy at war with its own system, or with those who would respect your policy and obey your laws? Should it be with that absolutism that tolerates no freedom of speech, no licence of opinion, and which can grow strong only at the expense of your vigor, and can become dominant, only upon the ruins of republican liberty? Or shall that sympathy be extended to those, who, cherishing the Catholic religion, would mould its policy to the theory of our government, and would submit their system of rule to that modification which it must receive, from contact with institutions like ours? I cannot, as a legislator, nor would I have the State look with indifference on a controversy like this. On the one side is priesthood, panoplied with all its power over the pockets and consciences of its people, armed with the terrible enginery of the Vatican, seeking in open defiance of the policy and laws of the State, to wrest every inch of sacred ground from the control of the laity, property secured by their sweat and sacrifices, and to vest it in the solitary hands of a single Bishop, that he may close the door of the sanctuary, put out the fires upon its altar, and scourge by his disciplinary lash, every communicant, from its sacraments, ordinances and worship, who dares think a thought independent of his Spiritual Master. On the other hand, we see a band of men who have lived long enough in their adopted country, to have the gristle of their liberal opinions hardened into bone, men devoted to the church of their fathers, but who love the State to which they have sworn allegiance, and who respect its institutions, we see them resisting, with a heroism which would honor the age of heroes, unitedly, unwaveringly, in defiance of bulls of excommunication, from Bishop, Legate, and the Pope, every attempt to override our laws, and to establish on the soil of Freedom, the temporal supremacy of a priesthood.

Sir, the Muse of History, has rarely transscribed to her records, an act of heroism, surpassing that which was enacted at the church of St. Louis, in Buffalo, on the 10th of September 1854, when, after years of painful controversy with the highest authorities of the Papal Church, its congregation met its Bishop, to decide upon his *ultimatum*. That ultimatum was, that the congregation should elect trustees, to be selected by himself. In other words, he would allow the congregation to be the throne, but he was to be the *power behind it!* How did they meet this ultimatum? As martyrs, refusing to yield the tithe of a hair from their original position. And there stands to-day, a proud monument of the devotion of that people to a true citizenship, that magnificent edifice, as for five years it has been, under the curse of the Bishop. There, still floats over its tower, the black flag, symbolical of the darkness which envelopes the altar over which it waves, bearing the significant inscription, "Where is our Shepherd?" That Church is the political Thermopylæ of the age.

Sir, these Catholic citizens of Buffalo, to-day appeal to the State through their representative, for protection in this, their fidelity. Urged to violate their oaths of allegiance to your laws, they have kept them inviolate. On which side, again I ask, shall the State be found—will it be with that power which exalts its head above the State, which makes obedience to you the signal for excommunication, and the fatal interdict! Aside from the question of justice, has the State no dignity to maintain? Were the question never so insignificant, it would be its duty to vindicate its authority, and to hedge up by legislation, against its indirect violation.

When it ceases to be sovereign, it sinks into contempt. No free State should tolerate, nor can it long survive, an *imperium in imperio*, which lives defiant of the civil power.

I propose, Sir, to submit a few considerations, why we should not second the policy of the Baltimore ordinance. To say nothing here of the political antagonisms of the Romish policy to our institutions, I would remark, that no clergy, of any denomination, or faith, should be vested with the power contemplated by that ordinance.

I yield to no man in a due respect for the spiritual office, but there is to be found in its very nature, a reason, why it should not be associated with temporal power. It was the result both of his observation, and his historical research, which led Lord CLARENDON to say, that "of all mankind none were so ill fitted for the management of affairs, as the clergy." Whenever invested with civil power, or with those elements of control outside of their influence as spiritual guides, which operate upon the consciences and pockets of men, they have as a class been the enemies of toleration, and when forming a part of the civil power of the State, the defenders of its abuses, and of its efforts to crush dissent and independency. Not to Catholic States alone need we go for the proofs, they are to be found in the history of the English Church, from Henry VIII, to the present century, and to every other era of clerical domination. The "CONVOCATION," an assembly of the established clergy, even after the Revolution of 1688, claimed to be independent of Parliament, and dictated to it a policy destructive of all toleration, save for the doctrines of the Establishment. Great as is the debt of gratitude due from the Christian world to WILLIAM OF ORANGE, for no one act of that great statesman, and true friend of civil liberty, is it more indebted, than for his final prorogation of that body.

The Corporation, and Test acts, which so long disgraced the Statutes of England, and the acts relating to Catholic disabilities, always found defenders in the established clergy. When Fox and Burke led the attacks in the British Parliament against these oppressive statutes, mitred Bishops entered the lists to oppose them, as if religion could not exist out of the Church. "*Episcopacy may fail, but religion exist,*" was the noble reply of Burke, and to a Protestant laity, is England indebted for the great triumph of religious liberty, secured by the repeal of those acts. Clergymen, naturally feel that they have charge of the most important of all possible interests, the souls of men. Confident of the truth of their own dogmas, and looking upon schism and dissent as fatal heresy, they are easily led to the belief, that it is their highest duty to bring all the enginery of the Church and the State, to crush out the first appearance of a revolt from their Church formulas and Church economics. If it be said, that this argument holds good only with the clergy of an established Church, I answer it is because an Establishment can invoke the aid of the civil power to compel conformity, and embarrass dissenters. The same element of intolerance, allow it development, exists in the bosom of every spiritual teacher.

But, I answer further, that in permitting a powerful Church to obtain the control, contemplated by this ordinance, which, where it may, invokes the civil arm to crush out all dissent from its faith, we cherish one of the most dangerous evils of an Establishment.

An Establishment, is a constituent element of the State, and aids in the formation of its laws, and gives tone, and shape, to its policy. So far as it can bring the co-ordinate branches of the government to adopt its views, so far, it is felt as a power, for weal or for woe. The danger to liberty, and the injustice to non-conformists, and to dissenters, consists in the *power to control*, and it is only dangerous as it possesses that power. But here, Sir, in the bosom of this free State, we find a Hierarchy, having no sympathies with our institutions, but in direct antagonism to the principles on which they rest, admitting no supreme fealty to the civil power, but acting under the impulsive energy of its Italian centre and head, not as a co-ordinate part of the government, but exalting itself above the State, and regulating its millions of Church property, utterly defiant of our policy, and our laws. It stands before us naked of apology, and can plead nothing, but the *sic volo*, of an usurped prerogative.

To favor the despotic control over the consciences of vast masses of our citizens, and consequently over their action, which the Baltimore policy would concentrate in a score or two of Bishops throughout the United States, leads to many of the evils of a union of Church and State. Our government seeks the disintegration of this power. The theory of the Catholic Church is, that it must be a unit, a unit in doctrine, a unit in practice. The Catholic priest, under the most liberal of systems, has a vast influence over his charge, by virtue of his office. Superadded to this, when he is invested with the power which the absolute proprietorship of all sacred places, can give him, when the altar belongs to the priest, when the Church and the Cathedral are his, where the Catholic hopes to worship while living, when the Cemetery is his, securing to him the keys of the consecrated grave, when the Hospital is his, admission to whose charities is upon the terms he shall dictate, when the Catholic Colleges, and other Seminaries of learning, are his, when the tens of millions of property, the donations of the Faithful, are all, the absolute proprietorship of the priest, have you not the elements of a "power in the State," whose harmlessness, rests only in its forbearance? Is it said that this power will not be exercised? That if tempted by some future Cataline to conspire against the liberties of the people, it will spurn the offer? Is this the lesson of history? So judged not our fathers who framed the first State Constitution, and who declared in letters which should be graven upon the American heart, as with "a pen of iron," that in founding the basis of free Empire, they "were" *required* to guard against "that spiritual oppression, and intolerance, wherewith the bigotry and ambition of weak and wicked priests, have scourged mankind." Distrust of power, is written all over our Constitution and our laws. The elements of power most provoking this distrust, were the spiritual, and the money power. The one was paralized, so far as was necessary to render it harmless, by establishing the freest license of religious sentiment, the right of dissent from any or all dogmas, the right of *revolt* from all Church economies, leaving responsibility for his faith, to the conscience of the citizen and to his God. Every new sect diminished this power, and thus schism, became an element of political security. Thus were drawn the teeth of the spiritual power. The money power was rendered harmless by our statute of distributions and of inheritance, by prohibiting the entailing of estates, by preventing accumulations in Corporations, by the process of distribution of that power rather than of its concentration. Our statute in relation to Religious Corporations, is one of the most marked and happy illustrations of this principle, where every member of each separate congregation, who contributes to the support of worship, has a voice in the control of the Church property, and a recognized proprietorship therein.

The Baltimore ordinance is the antagonism of all this. It abhors the policy of disintegration, and seeks the absolute control over the laity, by the concentration of the spiritual and temporal power, in the priesthood. Two millions of Catholic communicants in the United States, and probably thirty millions of consecrated property, and all, under the absolute control of perhaps fifty Bishops, and they, acknowledging allegiance to a foreign and absolute Potentate! Continue this policy for fifty years, when the Catholic population shall be twenty-five millions, and the property of the fifty Bishops, almost beyond computation, and I venture to say, that the Church, represented in its ecclesiastics, will be stronger than the government, and will dictate the terms of its existence! The crushing weight of such a power can be lifted only by the strong hand of Revolution. All the statutes of Mortmain, which English Parliaments could devise, did not save the necessity of the confiscation of the estates of the Catholic Clergy, to save the ascendency of the Crown. France affords another illustration. It was a corrupt priesthood, enriched at the expense of labor, which bolstering up the Bourbon throne, with it, as an ally, ground the million masses to powder. Church exactions and State oppressions, were the wrongs, which exorcised from the deeps of popular rage, the Genius of Revolution, which swept, as with iron hail, every vestige of regal, and ecclesiastical rule from the land. The Triumvirate rode the whirlwind, and for a time, guided the storm, but they did not create them. They were the natural offspring of abuses in Church and in State.

Mexico, is to-day a living illustration of the tendency of Church accumulations, when unrestrained by law. It is almost literally, the proprietorship of the Catholic Church. And there, the heavings of one revolution have hardly subsided, before we feel the convulsive throes of another. New York is not without her experience of the evils of large landed estates, acquired before the Revolution. The original crown grants to Trinity Church, and which, if vested rights cannot be disturbed, are constant objects of jealousy and distrust. Even now the question of submitting their titles to judicial scrutiny is urged to the legislature as a great measure of public policy.

The accomplished Attorney General (Ogden Hoffman) whom I now see before me—is already instructed to bring them before the judicial tribunals.

The large landed estates in some of our Eastern counties, have in late years led to revolutionary excesses alike reproachful and perilous. So much opposed are they to the spirit of our institutions, that their proprietors have felt compelled to compromise their legal rights, and to take steps looking to an entire surrender, upon considerations agreed upon by parties interested, of their feudal tenures and policy. Our last State Constitution, has carefully guarded against the possibility of the introduction into the State, of this system of tenantry.

There is another reason of State, why the control of Church property should be in the laity.

Our government is anomalous. It depends for its security, upon the development of the higher elements of the individual man. It places upon him, the responsibility of rule. If he be the slave of a priesthood, the first political allegiance of his heart, whether he be a native or an adopted citizen, will be elsewhere than to the government which protects him. If he surrender a portion of his franchise to his spiritual teacher, he will soon be prepared to surrender all his judgment, all his political individuality, to the same ambition.

The consciousness of that independence of spiritual control, which proprietorship in sacred places creates, is one of the processes of development of individual manhood, which the State cannot afford to surrender. Property is power. The State has a positive interest in retaining that element of influence in hands, where its possession will lead to attachment and fealty to its government. The people should trace their right to worship in consecrated places, built by their own sacrifices, to the government, which would by its beneficence, win the affections of its citizens, and not to an ecclesiastic, who will make blind submission to his authority, the terms of spiritual consolation, and of admission to consecrated ground.

There is another consideration, why the clergy should not step out of their sphere as spiritual teachers, affecting themselves. The purity of the clergy, depends upon their separation from the secularizing tendencies of politics and power. There can be no just respect for that office, when associated with secular affairs. They are not above the reach of temptation. Their preservation from demoralization, depends upon their seclusion from the paths of ambition. We are not without examples which should ever be as a waving sword between them, and the avenues to temporal power. "I have chosen you, twelve," said the Savior of the world, "and one of you, is a devil."—MAMMON,

> The least erected spirit, that fell
> From Heaven——

was the seducer of JUDAS.

The thirty pieces of silver, have paved the road to infamy, for many of the successors, of the betrayer of his Lord.

The Romish Church, is not without its distinguished examples of spiritual death, through the influence of a grasping ambition.—WOLSEY,

> That once trod the ways of glory,
> And sounded all the depths and shoals of honor,

on the exposure of his schemes to compass the power of the throne, and "gain the Popedom," uttered to his faithful Cromwell, a sentiment which the poet has invested with the charm of his genius, but without the slightest addition to its truth, or its power.

> Cromwell, I charge thee, fling away ambition,
> By that sin fell the angels. How can man then,
> The image of his Maker, hope to win by 't?

What wonder, that this poor Cardinal, who was glad to beg a little earth for charity, that he might lay down his weary bones and die, should exclaim in view of his fall,

> ———— O Cromwell, Cromwell,
> Had I but served my God, with half the zeal
> I served my King, he would not in mine age,
> Have left me, naked, to mine enemies.

It is the history of the Church in every age, that its purest examples, and most eminent piety, were among those who literally, went "about their master's business," entirely separate from the objects of ordinary ambition.

The general argument I have pressed would hold good, in relation to any body of ecclesiastics; the evils of the policy of placing this power in a priesthood, are incident to the system, whatever may be the spiritual character, or relations of the clergy, who may be vested with the power I have deprecated. But there is another view of this subject to be taken, which looks to the peculiar danger to our Institutions, which will grow from the union of the spiritual and temporal power, in the Catholic Priesthood. And that I may not be misunderstood, I wish here to say, that all I have said, or may say hereafter, in relation to the Catholic policy, and the danger involved in it, is confined entirely to the politics of that Church, and not to its mere doctrines of religious faith. With them I have nothing to do. I have no controversy with a man who worships saints, and believes in the "real presence." I have no doubt there is a road to Heaven through the Catholic Church. I may think much or little, of a Congress of Bishops from the ends of the world, who shall meet in the Seven Hilled City, and sit for days at the feet of the Papal See, resolving the "immaculate conception of the Virgin." It may not accord with my views, of what themes should in the middle of the nineteenth century, occupy so wise a body, but certainly it is a harmless discussion, and may be, a harmless fath. I have to do with a policy, other than mere dogmas of this character.

A law which shall prohibit the accumulation of property in the hands of the Catholic Bishops, I deem vitally necessary as a measure of safety to our political Institutions.

We cannot neglect to impose these legislative restraints, and take care that the State suffer no detriment. A popular government may still be an experiment, and time, under the happiest influences that human wisdom can devise, may prove their fatal tendency to decay, and dissolution. But we, sir, as a people, are committed to this experiment. All our character as a nation, all our pride in past achievement, all our confidence in present security, all our hopes of future glory, are concentrated in the hopeful capacity of intelligent man, for self-government. We are bound to give this experiment a fair trial, to protect it in all constitutional ways, against every influence adverse to its success. The political theory of the Catholic Hierarchy is in direct antagonism to the republican principle. Its theory is, that the individual man, is absorbed in the Catholic religionist, and the religionist, in the Head of the Church. The first allegiance of the true Catholic, according to the theory, is to the Papal power, his allegiance to human governments, entirely subordinate. This doctrine is as boldly avowed in this country, as it is in Rome. One of the most carefully written papers of Mr. Brownson, in his Catholic Review, a gentleman of high endowments, and who has recently in an appointment to a Professorship in a Catholic University, received the highest evidence of Catholic confidence, in speaking of this doctrine of allegiance, employed this language:

"If the Church should direct the Catholic citizens of this American Republic to abolish the Constitution, the liberty, and the very existence of their country, as a sovereign state, and transfer it to the crown of Louis Napoleon Bonaparte, they are bound, by a Divine ordinance, to obey.

"We are not aware of a single Catholic sovereign in modern history, that has regarded religion in any other light than as a branch of the police, although several of them have been personally pious. As princes, they have asserted the total separation of the two orders, and in their public and official conduct, have looked upon the Church merely as the auxiliary of the government, and religion as subordinated to the interests of the State. It is to this fact, that we must attribute the frightful scandals of Catholic Europe, for the last two centuries. The revolt and opposition of the Protestant nations of Europe, in the sixteenth century, and the wars which followed for over a hundred years, enabled the Catholic sovereigns to assert their independence, in temporals, of the spiritual power, to suppress the estates and to establish their absolute power.

This principle and its most natural illustration, are found in a recent number of the *Civila Catallica*, published at Rome, and the immediate organ of the Pope. That paper, of date 5th August, 1854, submits the following to the world: "That excommunication by the Church, has, as an unavoidable result, the dissolution of the tie of subjection and of the oath of fidelity."

I take the liberty of quoting the language of the New York *Tribune*, commenting upon the declaration, and which well says: "According ' to this, if a Pope should lay his ban upon the " government of the United States, Catholic " subjects of that government, would become " *ipso facto*, absolved from all fidelity thereto."

This, Sir, is the theory, and in accordance with it, is all their discipline, even their oaths of office, pledge to this policy all their spiritual teachers.

Now what is the position of affairs in this country. We have two million Catholics, ministered to by hundreds of priests. Who are these Catholics? The great mass of them are foreigners, many of them from the most absolute governments, governments in which the Catholic religion is the religion of the State, where the political education of the church, has been, that blind submission to the spiritual and the political power, is the duty of the true Catholic. Through this mutual support of the Hierarchy by the government, and of the government by the Hierarchy, through its control over the Catholic conscience, the absolute element in European politics has been maintained. Revolution has slumbered—the Church has administered the narcotics. Who are the spiritual teachers of our Catholic citizens? A native clergy? No sir, the native is the exception to the rule, almost universal. The Catholic priesthood of this country are generally foreigners, educated in the most absolute doctrines of Papal supremacy, who have no faith in human progress, who regard the doctrine of individual independence, as heresy. From necessity, they are the enemies of Republican Institutions. Why is this? Republican Institutions favor the right of private judgment. They invite the individual to break away from a blind submission to his spiritual guide, and to repose his conscience in the keeping of his God. They deny the supremacy of the Pope, and demand to the government, the first political allegiance of the citizen. Hence their whole policy, is to disintegrate that power, which the church is permitted to wield, in despotisms.

Should the State look with indifference upon this foreign control of this vast mass of mind, educated in this doctrine of blind obedience to a power that assumes to be superior to the State?

Whatever of influence the Clergy can retain through their office as teachers, while acting in conformity with our systems of polity, which are themselves adapted for general safety, is well. But it is madness in the State, to permit a policy, the antagonism of its own, to obtain, and which tends to weaken the tie of citizenship, while it builds up an overshadowing power of money and influence, all of which, is under the control of the most absolute Potentate on the earth.

Why was this ordinance of Baltimore enacted, tranferring the consecrated property of two millions of American citizens, to a half hundred foreign priests? Why was this policy adopted for free America, which can exist no where, except with the most absolute governments of Europe? Sir, it was a stroke of policy worthy of the conception of a HILDEBRAND, far seeing, appreciative of the contagious character of our institutions, and of their influence on the American Catholic mind. No wonder, it met the approval of the Roman Pontiff. That policy, perhaps the confession is indiscreet, but I do not purpose any concealments in what I have to say, was necessary, to retain the absolute ascendency of their priesthood, over the Catholic communion. Nothing short of this concentration of power and influence, could retain in blind subservience, a generation of Catholics born under our government. He would be comparatively a wise man, who should hope to press down with the palm of his hand the heavings of the Volcano, or by a word to appease the Spirit of the storm, as it rides forth on the blast, to him who should hope for the birth and education under our republican system, of a generation of men, of a foreign parentage, who would bear the yoke of priestly rule as tamely as did their fathers. There is contagion in the spirit of liberty. Undoubtedly that "abuse," spoken of in the Baltimore ordinance, which consists in a claim on the part of the laity to be represented in the temporal power of the Church, and to seek its adaptation to our own general system of rule, did exist, even as early as 1829. That it now exists, to a degree which threatens to weaken the power of the clergy, over matters not legitimate to them, is evidenced between the laity and the priesthood, in almost every State of the Union. Not in the Church of Buffalo alone, is found this spirit of *protest* against the absolute claims of the clergy. The Church of St. Peters of Rochester, is in the same controversy, and other congregations, I understand, in the city of Troy, in New York, in Cincinnati, in Louisville, in Detroit, indeed all over the country, either covertly, or openly, are to be found in the Catholic mind, the workings of the republican leaven. I do not mean by this, that any revolution is in progress, in relation to mere theologic questions. I believe there are none, but the controversy is purely in relation to questions of control, and of limitation of the clerical power, to their office, as spiritual teachers.

But the Church will answer me, that unless the priest control the altar, there is danger of schism, and that it will invite their people to protest, against Church dogmas, and Church polity. I would reply, that this is the land of dissent, that its institutions tolerate and invite dissent, that they were founded by those who were said by England's most philosophic statesman, to have embraced a religion which was the very "dissidence of dissent," and that its government cannot employ itself in forging chains for the human mind, or fetters for the conscience. On the contrary, it encourages research, it is hopeful, not fearful, of schisms, growing out of enlightened inquiry, in all questions of policy or faith. Its distrust is of the individual. Its confidence is in the species. In an earlier day, when were urged to Parliament the same reasons for forbiding the publication of dissenting opinions, MILTON, that

Great orb of song,

uttered a sentiment worthy of him, and of his age, and which is expressive of the confidence of the spirit of American democracy. "When "the cheerfulness of the people is so sprightly "up, that it has not only wherewith to guard "well its own freedom and safety, but to spare, "and to bestow upon the solidest and sublimest "points of controversy, and new invention, it "betokens us not degenerated, nor drooping to a "fatal decay, by casting off the old and wrinkled "skin of corruption, to outlive these pangs, and "wax young again, entering the glorious ways of "truth and prosperous virtue, destined to become "great, and honorable in these latter ages."

Was it not our country, upon which the prophetic vision of his mind rested, in that sublime rhapsody, when even his genius, was kindled with unwonted fires.

"Methinks I see in my mind, a noble, and "puissant nation, rousing herself like a strong "man after sleep, and shaking her invincible "locks. Methinks I see her as an eagle, mewing "her mighty youth, and kindling her undazzled "eyes at the full mid-day beam, purging and "unscaling her long abused sight, at the foun-"tain itself, of heavenly radiance, while the "whole noise of timorous and flocking birds, "with those also that love the twilight, flutter "about, amazed at what she means, and in their "envious gabble, would prognosticate a year of "sects and schisms."

No sir, the Catholic Hierarchy cannot ask our government to aid in perpetuating its venerable dogmas, of faith, or its hoary political abuses. The day has past in all governments, embodying in any considerable degree the popular element, which regards the plea of *prescription* in behalf of ancient opinions, errors, or systems. The age is a living demurrer to this defence.

Our government has but one reply to this cry of alarm that in republicanising the system of rule, over Church temporalities, we weaken the tie between the priest and the people, and invite to independency and dissent.

Being a government of dissent, and popular in all its theory, it cannot be moulded to meet more absolute systems of rule. It admits the transplantation to its soil of every exotic, spiritual or political, that can find it genial to its nature. Whether they are so, and can bear the transplantation, or whether they languish and die, is of no interest to the Genius of American Democracy. Its office is spent, when it has taken care that the State suffer no detriment, and that there spring up in its midst, no hostile element of power.

I know the Catholic priesthood have no sympathy with these sentiments, nor with the spirit of the age, which generates them. They as stoutly deny the rights we claim for their people as they did under the iron rule of the GREGORIES. Upon every other system which has come in contact with modern civilization, more or less impression has been made, modifying their severe features, and conforming them to the more liberal policy of the age. But the Procrustean bed of Catholic politics remains, unchanged. In the crucible of the Centuries, its system of rule has undergone no transmutation. It took Anglo Saxon Protestantism, but about one century, to work out its illiberality and intolerance. It did not spring like Minerva from the head of Jupiter, a complete creation from its birth. In Old England and in new, its origin was marked by the sentiment of a persecuting age, and blood was found upon its garments. But it bore within itself the elements of its own purgation, and today, it stands before the world regenerated from its intolerance, and full panoplied in all the elements of a liberal civilization. It has a free press, and open Bible, an universal education and a tolerant government. It takes struggling humanity by the hand, and leads it up to the heights of personal character. It leaves man, not a blind worshipper at the outer door, but invites him to the inner shrine of great Nature's Temple, and to be himself, as a priest, in the service of Truth and of God. Such, is in the middle of the 19th century, that Genius of REVOLT against abuses of Church and of State, named PROTESTANTISM. One more general view of this subject.

Catholic States, consistent in their theory, that heresy is crime, and should be crushed out by penalties and by death, close the doors against all protest, and even banish to exile or to death all who defy the omnipotent authority of the Church. It is to be remembered that while Spain and Portugal, are Catholic countries, that ours is a Protestant country, and in its highest sense, a Protestant government. I know the State as such, recognizes no religion as peculiarly its own. But in its sympathy, in its tone, in its spirit, and in its origin, it is Protestant. What constitutes a country? Surely not that alone which belongs to its physical, but that which pertains to its moral, its social, its intellectual, its political character. It is found in its civilization, in its sentiments, in its heart-enthroned prejudices, which have themselves become principles, guiding stars of a people's thought, and the impelling power to a nation's action. Judged by this standard, ours is a Protestant country, and a Protestant government. Protestantism for the most part formed its early settlement. Protestantism laid the basis of our State and National Institutions. A Protestant laity, independent in political action of priestly control, infused into all our policy, that liberal leaven which has given the utmost freedom to religious opinion and worship, and enabled even the Catholic Hierarchy, to grow so dominant in our midst. The Catholic clergy and their Italian head, have no claim upon our comity, to sacrifice a national policy to a trans-Atlantic system, the direct antagonism of our own.

It is proper before concluding my remarks, to analyze a little more particularly, the bill under consideration

The first section, seeks to invalidate future conveyances to priests and bishops, in their official character. It would prevent the evils of permitting ecclesiastics to become in fact, corporations sole, with power to acquire lands in perpetuity.

The second section, invalidates all future conveyance of lands consecrated or appropriated or intended so to be, to purposes of religious worship, unless made to a religious, corporation organized under our laws. This is to prevent the future acquisition of that class of property, in the hands of individual priests.

The third section, seeks to execute a moral trust, wherever such a trust exists, in the hands of individuals, by declaring that property, of the character named in the second section, shall be deemed to be held in trust for the benefit of the congregation using the same, and shall vest in their corporations after the decease of the person holding the legal title. In this respect, it is analagous to our statute of Uses and Trusts, by turning a trust estate into a legal estate, and vesting the absolute title in the party having the equitable interest.

Section four, declares that the property shall escheat to the State, on the decease of the party holding the legal title, unless the congregation should so far conform to our system and laws, as to organize into a corporation.

Section five, recognizes this estate so vesting by escheat in the people, as a moral trust, and provides for the conveyance of the property to the Trustees of the society, using the same, whenever the society shall organize into a corporation.

The whole object of these latter provisions, is to compel bishops and priests, of whatever denomination, Protestant if such there be, or Catholic, to permit the incorporation of their Societies, in order to pretect their titles. If they will not obey the laws of the land, will not conform to its policy, they are without the pale of, and have no claim on its protection, in relation to this class of property.

I would, in passing, remark that even with the free consent of their congregations, the State ought not to permit so insecure a trust of so vast possessions. The want of a subscribing witness to a will, or some other statute informality, not to name the possibility of an intentional error, would transfer the entire consecrated property in the diocese in the Catholic connection, to the next of kin to the bishop. The remedy for so great an outrage, would exist only in the free will of those, in whom the laws of inheritance should vest the title.

This is not novel legislation. Both it, and its occasion, have their counterpart. Let us look for a moment into the iron visage of the Past, and see in it the reflex image of our Present.

The spirit of English liberty was ever jealous of priestly prerogative. Having the sole control over spiritualities, the Catholic clergy were in the middle ages, as now, active in securing the same centralization in themselves, of temporal power. They understood the philosophy of human nature well enough to know, that the possession of the physical wealth of the State, would greatly facilitate their attainment of all other desirable influence. Through this, the church could control the consciences of the people, and the policy of Kings. Hence it was, that in the darkest hour of the middle ages, when the English throne scarce had a being save at the pleasure of the Roman Pontiff, nearly one-half the real estate of the kingdom was absorbed in the Catholic Church. The Church was every thing, royalty but its shadow. The spirit of English liberty, whenever it incited revolt against abuses, attacked the grasping element of the Papal Hierarchy, and it never felt that it had achieved a substantial victory which did not diminish that overshadowing power—and prevent its acquisition of real estate. So vital was this regarded, so essential to the liberty of the citizen, that it was provided in *magna charta* itself, that great bill of rights of Englishmen, that lands should not thereafter be given in *mortmain* to religious houses—that is, to remain forever from ordindry use and alienation. This statute was evaded by the clergy through the system of leasing lands, to prevent which, was passed the statute of 1 Edward *de viris religionis*, (concerning priests,) which forfeited to the crown, lands taken in mortmain. The following is a copy of this provision:

"No person, religious or other whatsoever body politic, ecclesiastical or lay, sole or aggregate, shall buy or sell any lands or tenements, or under the color of gift or lease, or by reason of any title receive the same, or by any other craft or engine, shall presume to appropriate to himself, whereby such lands may in any wise come into mortmain, under pain of forfeiture of the same. And within the year after the alienation, the next lord of the fee may enter. And if he do not, then the next immediate lord from time to time to have half a year, and in default of all the mesne lords entering, the king shall have the lands so alienated forever, and shall enfeoff others by certain services."

This was again evaded by false actions, and judgments obtained by collusion, whence titles called *common recoveries*, which was met by another statute, in the same reign. The next device to evade the statute, was by conveying lands in *trust* for the *use* of the clergy, to meet which, Parliament passed an act of forfeiture in the reign of Richard II., unless held by consent of the King. The compulsory feature of nearly all the English Acts of mortmain consists in the forfeiture of the lands to the Crown, which were grasped by the clergy in violation of the policy, and law of the land.

The last general English statute on this subject, passed in the reign of George II., as well as the statute of 43 Elizabeth, specially designates what grants and devises shall be lawful for charitable uses, and invalidates every conveyance and devise not authorized by those Acts. To watch the clergy, has been the business of Parliaments, to save their lands, from mortmain, the business of the people, for centuries past, well is it, if it be not so, for centuries to ccme.

The great end to be attained by this bill, as I have argued at length, is to divest the clergy of the power of control over Church temporalities. The only modification of this bill I have heard suggested, authorizes the Bishop of the Diocese to appoint three trustees, should the congregation decline to avail themselves of their legal privileges of incorporation. This would, in my judgment, leave the evil almost untouched. The result would be, that that discipline which has compelled so many congregations to surrender their charters, would be brought to bear upon them, to compel them to waive their rights under the bill, and allow the Bishop to select his own trustees. This was the very point which Bishop Timon was at last prepared to yield to the Church of St. Louis. Of course the Bishop would in every instance, select the most facile instruments, who would be invested with a nominal authority, but leaving the control still absolute in himself. To resist his will, would require as much fortitude then, as now, and how few congregations, but would endure almost any privation, rather than suffer as all resisting Catholic congregations have suffered. I take the liberty of reading an extract from a letter addressed to me by an eminent Catholic, and a trustee of the Church of St. Louis, in Buffalo, bearing witness to these persecutions. He says:

"In the United States of late years, the Arch "Bishops, and Bishops setting their will above "the laws, met in a synod at Baltimore, and "adopted a decree, by which no Church was to "be consecrated, if not previously deeded to "the Arch-Bishop or Bishop in whose Diocese it "was situated! Not satisfied with that awful "step, they declared an unrelenting war against "all the incorporated Catholic congregations, "and by incessant demands, threats, all kinds of religious deprivations, and lastly by excom-"munication, succeeded in destroying those law-"ful associations.

"In Buffalo, there is now but the St. Louis "Catholic Church which is incorporated, but to "what religious deprivation have they not been "condemned by their Bishop, for their resistance "to his will! Their priests taken away from "their Church, the congregation deprived of re-"ligious marriage, the sick of the holy sacra-"ments, and their trustees excommunicated!! "Indeed, it is no wonder after so much suffering, "that so many Catholic congregations should "have submitted to their Bishops in annulling "their charters and deeding their Churches to "them."

Says the Nuncio, Bedini, in his farewell letter to the Church of St. Louis, "The Bishop does "not ask for himself the administration, he is "ready to place it in the hands of members of "your own congregation, but *appointed by him*."

In his farewell letter to Bishop Timon, in alluding to the "obstinacy" of the congregation, he foreshadows the awful denunciations to which they have been subjected. "I consider them as not being Catholics at heart, and Rt. Rev. Sir, should your episcopal ministry inspire you to declare so, *in any way*, in order that good Catholics may know who are their brethren and who are not, I leave it to your discretion, and to your holy inspirations." So much for the former Governor of Bologna, and his tender mercies, alike tender to the brave Ugo Bassi, in whom were rekindled the ancient patriotism and genius of Italy, and to the persecuted Church of St. Louis.

How do the horrors of the fatal "Interdict" rush upon our minds as we read of this conflict between the people and the priest!

Wordsworth's sonnet was written of another age and country, but its application is not all inappropriate to Republican America:

"Realms quake by turns, proud arbitress of Grace,
The Church, by mandate shadowing forth the power
She arrogates o'er Heaven's eternal door,
Closes the gates of every sacred place.
Straight from the Sun and tainted air's embrace,
All sacred things are covered, cheerful morn
Grows sad as night, no seemly garb is worn,
Nor is a face allowed to meet a face
With natural smile of greeting. Bells are dumb,
Ditches are graves, funeral rites denied,
And in the church yard he must take his bride,
Who dares be wedded. Fancies thickly come
Into the pensive heart, ill-fortified,
And comfortless despairs the soul benumb."

I cannot resist the impulse to read one additional paragraph from the same letter, expressing the sentiment of a vast body, of intelligent Catholics throughout the land. He says:

"It is highly time that the Legislature should "cast an eye of commisseration and protection "upon us by the adoption of a law, putting a "stop to the encroachments of the Bishops and "Catholic clergy in general, specifying that all "Church property should only be possessed by "their right owners, the people who have paid "for them." I will only add, that this is but one of many similar expressions I have received from the Catholic laity of different congregations in the State. And has it come to this, that the Catholic laity of our State, implore its Legislature to "commisserate and protect" them from ecclesiastical outrage? Will New York refuse this protection? They have asked for bread will she give them a stone? They have asked that she maintain the spirit of her own laws will she allow it to be borne down by the despotic policy of a priesthood?

I said in the outset of my remarks, that this bill struck at no universal practice of the Church.

In France, the temporal administration of the Church is in the council of *Fabrique* (Board of Trustees) who are chosen by the muncipal council, the latter being elected by the people in the several communes. In part of the German States, Belgium and other parts of the continent which have been under the French domination the Catholic temporalities are administered in the same manner, by laymen. The same exists in Switzerland.

In France, the clergy cannot accept donations by will or otherwise for any benevolent establishment, without the sanction of the government and then to be under the control of the civil power.

Thus it will be seen, that the policy which has confiscated twenty-five millions of property, belonging to two millions of American citizens, to a half hundred priests, whose first allegiance is to the Papal See, is a policy especially reserved for Republican America! This offshoot of Absolutism, which can flourish nowhere outside of Spain and Portugal, where deceased Protestants are buried like dogs, if buried at all, where the torch of persecution is ever lighted, has been transplanted, has grown, and flourished, on the soil of Freedom! This is the political paradox of the age. It is deeply implanted, and already begins to overshadow the State. But one question is unsolved, will you now lay the legislative axe to the root of this Upas, or will you leave it to be uptorn at a future day, by the storm of Revolution?

www.ingramcontent.com/pod-product-compliance
Lightning Source LLC
LaVergne TN
LVHW020643110826
845149LV00004B/1341

* 9 7 8 1 4 1 8 1 8 9 6 1 7 *